Where People Work

What Happens at a
Dairy Farm?

by Kathleen Pohl

Reading consultant: Susan Nations, M.Ed., author/literacy coach/consultant in literacy development

Please visit our web site at: www.garethstevens.com
For a free color catalog describing Weekly Reader® Early Learning Library's list
of high-quality books, call 1-877-445-5824 (USA) or 1-800-387-3178 (Canada).
Weekly Reader® Early Learning Library's fax: (414) 336-0164.

Library of Congress Cataloging-in-Publication Data

Pohl, Kathleen.
 What happens at a dairy farm? / by Kathleen Pohl.
   p. cm. — (Where people work)
 Includes bibliographical references and index.
 ISBN-10: 0-8368-6886-2 — ISBN-13: 978-0-8368-6886-9 (lib. bdg.)
 ISBN-10: 0-8368-6893-5 — ISBN-13: 978-0-8368-6893-7 (softcover)
 1. Dairy cattle—Juvenile literature. 2. Cows—Juvenile literature.
 3. Dairying—Juvenile literature. I. Title. II. Series.
 SF208P64   2007
 637—dc22   2006007674

This edition first published in 2007 by
Weekly Reader® Early Learning Library
A Member of the WRC Media Family of Companies
330 West Olive Street, Suite 100
Milwaukee, Wisconsin 53212 USA

Managing editor: Dorothy L. Gibbs
Art direction: Tammy West
Cover design and page layout: Scott M. Krall
Picture research: Diane Laska-Swanke and Kathleen Pohl
Photographer: Jack Long

Acknowledgments: The publisher thanks Tondra Fox, Ralph Gehl, and Paul Hurtgen for their kind
assistance. Special thanks to Adaijah Oliver for modeling in this book and to Robert Winkelmann
for his expert consulting and the use of his farm's facilities.

Printed in the United States of America

1 2 3 4 5 6 7 8 9 10 09 08 07 06

Hi, Kids!

I'm Buddy, your Weekly Reader® pal. Have you ever visited a dairy farm? I'm here to show and tell what happens at a dairy farm. So, come on. Turn the page and read along!

Don't you just love a cold glass of milk? Most of the milk we drink comes from cows. Milk cows live on **dairy** farms. The farmer keeps the cows inside a big barn.

Cows with black and white spots are **Holsteins**. Dairy farmers like this **breed**, or kind, of cows. Holsteins give lots of milk!

A cow cannot give milk until after she has her first calf. Can you tell that this calf is a Holstein?

Dairy cows need to eat lots of food to make lots of milk! The farmer feeds his cows hay. Cows also eat grain.

Now it is milking time! First, the farmer washes the cow's **udder**. The cow's milk is stored in the udder.

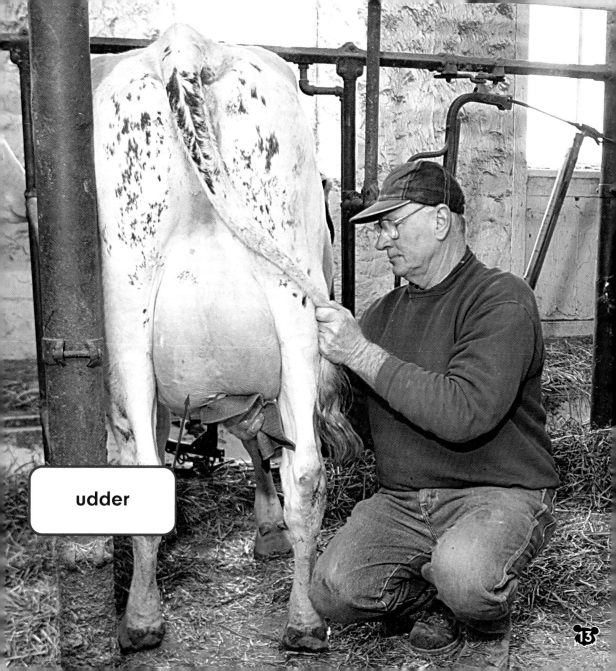

udder

13

Next, the farmer attaches a **milking machine** to the udder. This machine sucks out the warm milk.

milking machine

15

The milk goes right from the machine to a big tank in the **milk house**. The tank stores milk from all the cows. It cools the milk, too.

tank

milk

17

Later, the milk truck comes. It takes the milk to a dairy plant. The milk will be **bottled** at the dairy plant.

Mmmm . . . Milk tastes so good — especially with a cookie!

🐻 Glossary

bottled – put into bottles

breed – a group of animals that look and act alike in many ways

dairy – milk or milk products, such as butter and cheese

grain – the seeds of cereal plants, such as wheat, corn, and oats

Holsteins – dairy cows that are black and white

udder – the baglike part of a cow's body where the cow's milk is stored

🐻 For More Information

Books

Dairy Plant. Read and Learn (series).
  Angela Leeper (Heinemann Library)

Milk. What's for Lunch? (series). Claire Llewellyn
  (Children's Press)

Web Sites

MooMilk
  www.moomilk.com
  Follow the story of milk — and have fun, too!

4-H Virtual Farm
  www.ext.vt.edu/resources/4h/virtualfarm/main.html
  Click on the cow to find out all about dairy farms.

Publisher's note to educators and parents: Our editors have carefully
reviewed these Web sites to ensure that they are suitable for children.
Many Web sites change frequently, however, and we cannot guarantee
that a site's future contents will continue to meet our high standards of
quality and educational value. Be advised that children should be closely
supervised whenever they access the Internet.

# Index

About the Author

Kathleen Pohl has written and edited many children's books. Among them are animal tales, rhyming books, retold classics, and the forty-book series *Nature Close-Ups*. She also served for many years as top editor of *Taste of Home* and *Country Woman* magazines. She and her husband, Bruce, live among beautiful Wisconsin woods and share their home with six goats, a llama, and all kinds of wonderful woodland creatures.